SPECIALS!

Basic Skills in English

Maureen Mills
Margaret Underhill

Folens
Publishers

Acknowledgements

© 1995 Folens Limited, on behalf of the authors.

First published 1995 by Folens Limited, Albert House, Apex Business Centre, Boscombe Road, Dunstable, LU5 4RL, England.

ISBN 1 85276 674-3   Printed by Craft Print Pte Ltd, Singapore

Editor: Catherine Miller
Illustrations: Eric Jones
Cover photo: The Image Bank
Layout Artist: Margaret Tindall

Contents

Basic Skills in English

Introduction

Because it is artificial to separate language and grammar, the activities in this book seek to develop skills without being pedantic or purist in approach.

The general aim of the activities is to improve the written text produced by pupils, especially those who are experiencing learning difficulties; the specific aims are, hopefully, self-evident.

The material falls broadly into three sections:

1. The basics (pages 5–27)
This deals with the technicalities of producing written work. Activity sheets are provided, dealing with sentence construction, paragraphing and story writing. A wide range of punctuation skills are addressed, including capital letters and full stops, commas, apostrophes and inverted commas. Attention is paid to the problems of writing and reporting conversations.

2. Grammar skills (pages 28–41)
This is concerned with putting 'colour' into the written work of pupils, as well as teaching more formal grammar. Activity sheets deal with nouns, verbs, adjectives, adverbs and conjunctions. They seek to correct some common errors and also to develop basic vocabulary skills. Activities encourage the correct use of tenses and person in storytelling. Similes, metaphors and alliteration are also dealt with.

3. Reading and proof-reading skills (pages 42–48)

This looks at a variety of approaches to reading, comprehension and proof-reading, including cloze procedure, sequencing text, letter writing and the use of more inferential material.

Although the activities aim to cover these three broad areas, all of the material does not naturally fall into these sections. Some sheets will cover more than one of these skills and the teacher should use his or her discretion about which area it is best to focus on with the individual child. This allows for a more flexible approach.

Careful attention has been paid to the appropriateness of reading and interest levels. Many pages include illustrations that help in the understanding of the text. The mix of activities ensures that provision can be made for independent and collaborative work. Many activities are designed with paired or group work in mind. One of the most successful ways of developing language skills in the classroom is in the context of small group work, where collaboration and discussion are encouraged.

'speech marks'

capital letters

commas

exclamation marks

full stops

Basic Skills in English

A sentence puzzle

Sentences

make sense   start with a capital letter   end with a full stop.

● Underline the sentences below. Write them in the box and solve the puzzle.

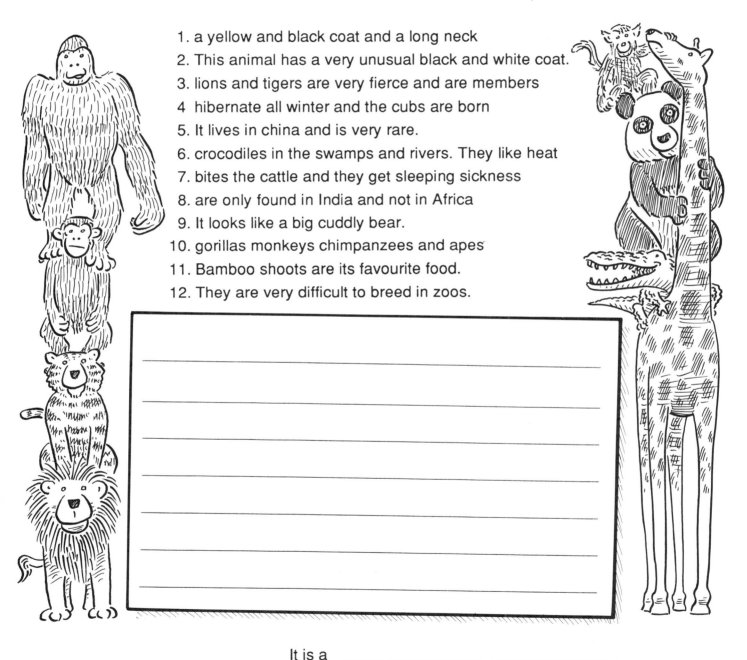

1. a yellow and black coat and a long neck
2. This animal has a very unusual black and white coat.
3. lions and tigers are very fierce and are members
4 hibernate all winter and the cubs are born
5. It lives in china and is very rare.
6. crocodiles in the swamps and rivers. They like heat
7. bites the cattle and they get sleeping sickness
8. are only found in India and not in Africa
9. It looks like a big cuddly bear.
10. gorillas monkeys chimpanzees and apes
11. Bamboo shoots are its favourite food.
12. They are very difficult to breed in zoos.

It is a _____

    ● Make up a puzzle like this one and test a partner.

Sentences

● Find the sentences in the passages below. Put in the full stops and capital letters and write the sentences on the lines.

lie down now its time to go to sleep in the morning we will go swimming at the shops they bought food for a picnic lunch was at 1.00 when the bell rang the fire engine came and rescued the cat stuck in the tree

1. _____

2. _____

3. _____

4. _____

5. _____

look at the birds flying is an expensive way to travel getting to work is very difficult when the buses are on strike action is to be taken about joyriders speeding in built-up areas is dangerous

1. _____

2. _____

3. _____

4. _____

5. _____

● Turn over and write five sentences about the picture below. Check your work using the **REMEMBER** rule.

Sentences and paragraphs

REMEMBER: Sentences must make sense.

● Underline the sentences in the examples below.

Australia is a huge country on the other side of the world.

It is so big you have to fly across it.

Many unusual animals like the kangaroo and koala bear

Children often do their school work at home and talk to the teacher by radio contact.

The men are supposed to be tough and drink a lot of lager.

The sheep farms are very big and if you are a farmer

It is very hot there and the centre of the country is desert.

Many popular TV programmes and entertainers and comics

● Pick two of the statements that did not make sense. Alter them so that they are sentences. Write them on the lines below.

_____

_____

● The sentences below are all about the same subject. What is the subject?

Sydney is the capital of New South Wales. It is the oldest town in Australia and has one of the finest harbours in the world. There are many important buildings in Sydney but the best known is the Opera House. There are many parks and open spaces. The people of Sydney are proud of their city.

 ● A group of sentences about the same subject or topic is called a paragraph. Turn over and write a paragraph about where you live.

Subject, verb, object

Most sentences have a **subject**, a **verb** and an **object**.

The cat **(subject)** ate **(verb)** the mouse **(object)**.
The nurse **(subject)** fed **(verb)** the child **(object)**.

You can improve your writing by adding information to each part.

The **sly, old** cat ate the **poor, skinny** mouse.
The **kind, young** nurse fed the **weak, little** child.

● Improve these sentences by adding to the subject and the object.

Subject	Verb	Object
The _____ rabbit	nibbled	the _____ shoots.
My _____ coat	kept out	the _____ wind.
Tom's _____ sister	ate	the _____ slugs.
The _____ boy	climbed on	the _____ roof.
Two _____ men	walked on	the _____ sand.
My _____ grandma	fell over	the _____ carpet.
The _____ thief	stole	the _____ jewels.
The _____ joy rider	crashed	the _____ car.
The _____ lesson	bored	the _____ class.
The _____ aeroplane	crashed in	the _____ mountains.

SUBJECT 〔 WHO? 〕 VERB 〔 DID WHAT? 〕 OBJECT 〔 TO WHAT OR WHOM? 〕

Basic Skills in English   © Folens

Better sentences, better stories

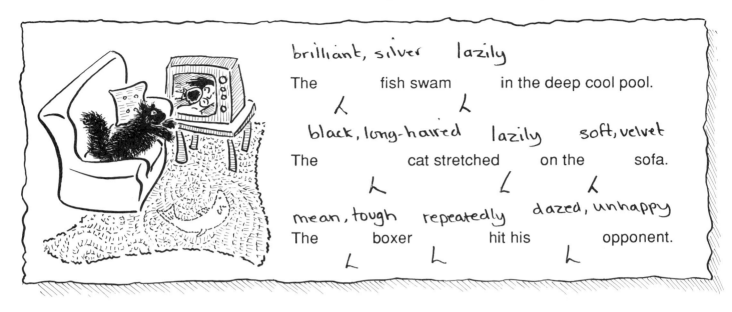

brilliant, silver   lazily

The   fish swam   in the deep cool pool.

black, long-haired   lazily   soft, velvet

The   cat stretched   on the   sofa.

mean, tough   repeatedly   dazed, unhappy

The   boxer   hit his   opponent.

- Now improve the three sentences below by adding detail.

1. The headmaster stood in the assembly and shouted at the children.

2. The football coach cheered her team as they came off the field.

3. The wind blew under the door and through the windows.

- Look at this picture of carnival day in Brazil.

It is hot, colourful and loud. There is music, dancing and steel bands. The way people dress is fantastic. Think of the colours, the noises and the smells.

- Imagine you are in Brazil. Write an account for the local paper at home.

Paragraphs

A group of sentences all about one topic is called a paragraph.

- The sentences below describe Ben.
  Write them, or their numbers, in the chart under the three headings.

1. Ben has long, dark brown, curly hair.

2. He enjoys swimming and water sports.

3. In his family there are two younger sisters and one baby brother.

4. His dad is a postman.

5. He dreams of being a scuba diver.

6. His mum works part-time at the supermarket.

7. He is the oldest child of the family.

8. He is tall for his age, compared to his friends.

9. Ben's eyes are large and dark brown.

10. Ben does not burn in the sun; he gets a good tan.

11. The local swimming baths run courses on snorkelling; Ben wants to go on one.

12. His mum is often tired and he sometimes meets the young ones from school.

13. He does a morning and evening paper round which could help pay for a snorkelling course.

Describing Ben's family	Describing Ben's looks	Ben's hobbies, likes and dislikes
		Continue over the page ...

- Write three paragraphs about Ben, one about each heading.

Basic Skills in English   © Folens

Paragraphs 2

- The report below is ready to go on a television news programme. Cut out the strips and put the paragraphs in order to make sense.
- Is there more than one right order?

Police would like to question two boys seen running away from the car park at the rear of Barclays Bank at 5.30pm yesterday.

The man was found slumped between the dustbins at the rear of the shopping centre. On arrival at hospital he was found to be suffering from cuts, bruising and concussion. He was wearing a dark grey suit, heavy woollen overcoat and black leather shoes. He had been beaten with a blunt instrument causing severe injuries to his head and face. His wallet had been stolen and there was no other form of identification.

Although the identity of the man is unknown at present, there are some clues. We think he could be a business man, because of the type of clothing he was wearing; also his hands were soft and the nails well cared for, therefore we do not think he is a manual worker. There was a bunch of keys found in a trouser pocket, including a set of car keys we believe for a Ford Mondeo. Police are making a special plea for anyone working in the shopping centre who may have had a meeting with this man yesterday.

The man shown in this picture is aged between 40–45 years old. He has no memory of the attack and also no memory of his name or address. He is recovering in Newtown General Hospital from a brutal assault. If anyone recognises him, please contact Newtown Police on 071 265434.

The unidentified man turned out to be _____ .
- Choose his identity and write a T.V. report explaining who he was and what happened next.

© Folens   *Basic Skills in English*   11

Paragraphs make stories

| Start | ➡ | Middle | ➡ | End |

- Plan a story about Saturday Night. Divide it into paragraphs.
- Write words as clues in each box.
- When you have your ideas, write your story in the 'Saturday Night' box.

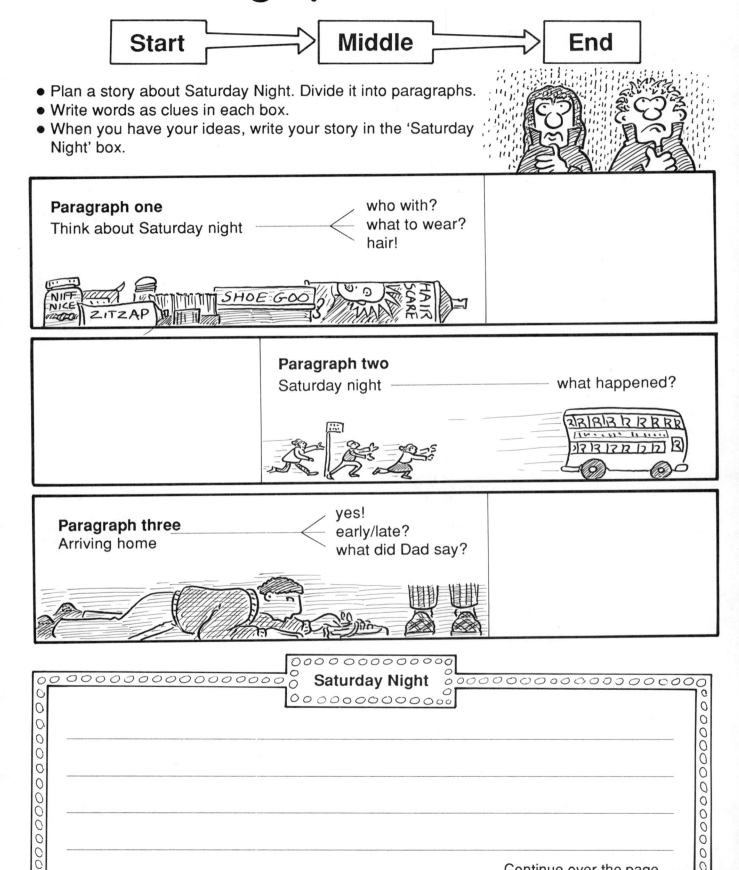

Paragraph one
Think about Saturday night —— who with?
what to wear?
hair!

NIFF NICE   ZITZAP   SHOE-GOO   HAIR SCARE

Paragraph two
Saturday night ——————————— what happened?

Paragraph three
Arriving home —— yes!
early/late?
what did Dad say?

Saturday Night

_____

_____

_____

_____

Continue over the page ...

Basic Skills in English   © Folens

Paragraphs make stories 2

Remember you need a *new* paragraph for each new part of a story.

● Write key words for each picture in the rocket.

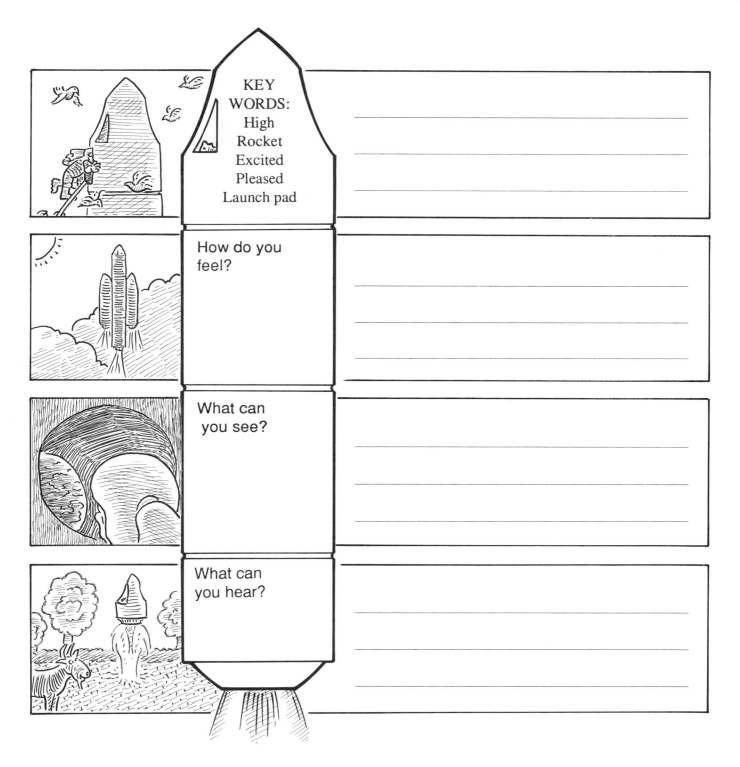

KEY WORDS:
High
Rocket
Excited
Pleased
Launch pad

How do you feel?

What can you see?

What can you hear?

 ● When you have your ideas, write the four paragraphs in the boxes.

Commas in lists

You use commas when you write lists.
You do *not* need a comma before the word '*and*' when it is at the end of a list.

Example: I bought an apple, two bananas, a grapefruit *and* six oranges.

● Write the commas in the two sentences below.

1. Taking the baby with us meant we needed a buggy nappies bottles and the car seat.

2. My sister spends hours in the bathroom. She takes a drink sweets books and a radio.

● Write a list of your favourite:

Foods	Football teams	Hobbies

● Write out your lists in sentences, remembering capital letters, commas and full stops.

I like . . .

Continue over the page ...

Basic Skills in English © Folens

Take a breath, use a comma

Commas (,) are used when you have to pause in a sentence.

Example: If I finish the washing, I might go for a swim this afternoon.

● Write the commas in the example below.

COMMATOWN HIGH SCHOOL

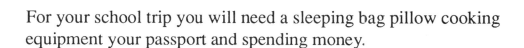

For your school trip you will need a sleeping bag pillow cooking equipment your passport and spending money.

You need to be at school by 7.00am on Sunday morning with all your luggage. No Walkmans allowed.

Our journey will start at 7.30am there will be a break at 11.00. We catch the 12.00 ferry and the crossing will take six hours arriving at 7.00pm hours local time.

When we arrive in Calais you will be told which family you will be staying with. You will need to collect your sleeping bag and rucksack please bring all waste paper drinks cans and other rubbish off the coach with you. Make sure that you have your passports and money ready as you will need to show your passports to the Customs Officials.

As you are staying with a family remember your manners and say 'please' and 'thank you'. In France if you ask for tea always ask for cold milk with it. You may prefer chocolate to coffee.

The French drive on the right so take care to look left right left when you need to cross the road.

 ● Go back and check your work with a partner.

Apostrophes

Apostrophes can show when a word has been shortened.

- Circle the letters that are left out when the short form is used.
- Write out the short form using an apostrophe.

sh(e + wi)ll	She'll	she + is	_____
can + not	_____	you + are	_____
they + have	_____	I + am	_____
he + is	_____	is + not	_____
we + have	_____	I + will	_____
they + will	_____	I + have	_____
they + are	_____	must + not	_____

NoW ☞ • Look at the passage below.

can't

I (cannot) help you now, (I have) too much work to do. Why not ask Gran or

Granddad? (They have) a lot more time than (I have) got. Granddad will be best

because (he has) a bad back so he (is not) doing any work in the garden. I

(must not) leave the washing any longer. Saturday is my only day off and (that is)

why (I am) trying to get all the housework done. (I will) be finished by tea time.

- Write it out, changing the words in brackets to the shortened form.

Basic Skills in English

Apostrophes 2

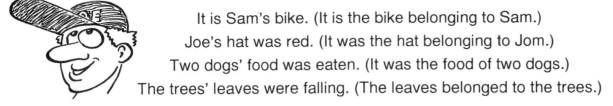

Apostrophes can show that something belongs to something or someone.

It is Sam's bike. (It is the bike belonging to Sam.)
Joe's hat was red. (It was the hat belonging to Jom.)
Two dogs' food was eaten. (It was the food of two dogs.)
The trees' leaves were falling. (The leaves belonged to the trees.)

● What do you notice about where the apostrophes are put?

● Read the passage below. Write in the apostrophes.
Think: are you reading about one or more?

The ships sails were full of the strong wind. The race was nearly

over, these sailors had been away for six months. The families and

other people watching were all cheering their favourite team. The

crowds yells were so loud that the policemans voice coming through

the loudspeaker was not heard.

Some people had brought young children sitting in buggies;

they could not see and got very cross. The childrens screams added

to the rest of the noise. A large dog had been tied to a post so that

his owner could go and watch the end of the race.

The noise scared him and the dogs barking made me give up. I

would see more on the television.

● Go back and check your work with a partner.

Basic Skills in English

Who said that?

COME ON, GALLOP, YOU LAZY, GOOD FOR NOTHING HORSE, *cried the fat lady.*

GALLOP WITH A BIG FAT LUMP LIKE YOU ON MY BACK? I CAN HARDLY WALK! *thought the horse.*

JOGGING KEEPS YOU FIT AND READY FOR ANYTHING, *said the jogger.*

I'M READY FOR MY DOG BISCUIT AND A LIE DOWN, *puffed the little dog.*

- Fill in the speech bubbles.

thought the gorilla.

said the young man.

thought the tiger.

said the woman.

- Turn over and write some more speech bubbles. Illustrate them.

NoW

Basic Skills in English

Speech marks

Instead of a speech bubble, use speech marks or 'inverted commas'.

● Write out the story below, use inverted commas.

Tom and William were in the park and along came Zach. "Oh here comes Zach. Let's not speak to him. We don't want him hanging on." said William.

Said .... said ... said ...

complained the teacher.

agreed Pam.

answered the policeman.

stammered the boy.

growled the park keeper.

shouted the referee.

not again ... not again ... not again ... not again

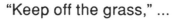

- Complete the sentences below. Do not use 'said'. Some of the pictures may help you.

"Keep off the grass," ...

"I was not pushing, it was not a foul," ...

"You are always wanting more money," ...

"Yes, you are right," ...

"You can't park here," ...

"Keep quiet, we don't want the police here," ...

"I do," ...

"If you don't want to buy anything, stop touching everything," ...

"This homework is a mess," ...

"I swear to tell the truth and nothing but the truth," ...

snapped the shop assistant.

recited the actor.

asked Glen.

warned the traffic warden.

giggled the girl.

replied the post lady.

whispered the thief.

smiled Anne.

laughed the comic.

moaned Dad.

repeated the vicar.

swore the prisoner.

- Make up five new sentences and write them below. Do not use 'said'.

Continued over the page ...

Basic Skills in English

Who said what?

- Talk about the differences in the following two ways of speaking.

Kevin and Tracey were talking.

"I'm going to the disco tonight, are you?" asked Kevin.

"No," moaned Tracey, "I'm not allowed to go."

- Change the picture story below to speech and write it out. Remember to start a new line for each new speaker.

Basic Skills in English

Questions and answers

Who are you?

_____

_____

_____

Where do you live?

_____

_____

_____

What are you doing here?

_____

_____

_____

Why do you
have a gun?

_____

_____

_____

- Write the answer to each question on the lines.
- Draw an interesting face in the box below and write the answers to the questions.

Who are you?

_____

_____

_____

Where do you
come from?

_____

_____

_____

How do you make
your living?

_____

_____

_____

What do you enjoy
doing best?

_____

_____

_____

- Choose a famous person and write an imaginary interview with them.
- Write the questions and then the answers.
- Remember to give each speaker a new line and use:

Who?   What?   Why?   Where?   When?   How?

Did you?   Have you?   Would you?

What did he or she say?

It is not always best to write a story using direct speech and inverted commas. Sometimes it makes a story faster and more exciting if you use reported speech.

- Look at the examples to see how it is done.

The doorman said, "You cannot come in without a tie."

or

The doorman said that he could not go in without a tie.

The bouncer warned, "If you make trouble you will be out."

or

The bouncer said that if they made trouble they would be out.

- Talk about the differences you notice in the two versions.
- Circle any changes in red.

 • Change the direct speech in the examples below to reported speech. Remember to ask yourself, "What did he or she say?"

1. "I am going to London to see a show," said Jenny.
2. "I have left the Scouts, I'm too old for that sort of thing," said William.
3. "We will be going out at seven so you must get home," warned Mum.
4. "Standing room only!" shouted the man on the gate.
5. "You handled the ball, so you are off," ordered the referee.
6. "If you are going to cook you had better wash your hands," suggested Mum.
7. "Don't cut too much off," said Damien to the hairdresser.
8. "If I don't eat something soon I will die," moaned Sally.

Reported speech

Interviews are 'reported', the news is 'reported', sports events are 'reported'.
Someone else reports what another person has said. Reported speech is in the past tense.

"If Bobby comes around here I will knock his head off," threatened the manager.

BECOMES

The manager said that if Bobby came around there he would knock his head off.

- Read the conversation below.
- Underline the verbs in red.
- Talk about what tense they are in.

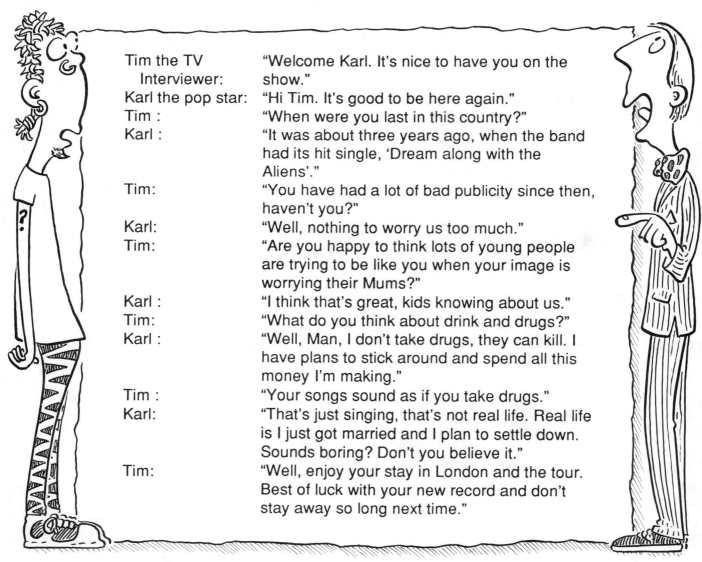

Tim the TV Interviewer:	"Welcome Karl. It's nice to have you on the show."
Karl the pop star:	"Hi Tim. It's good to be here again."
Tim :	"When were you last in this country?"
Karl :	"It was about three years ago, when the band had its hit single, 'Dream along with the Aliens'."
Tim:	"You have had a lot of bad publicity since then, haven't you?"
Karl:	"Well, nothing to worry us too much."
Tim:	"Are you happy to think lots of young people are trying to be like you when your image is worrying their Mums?"
Karl :	"I think that's great, kids knowing about us."
Tim:	"What do you think about drink and drugs?"
Karl :	"Well, Man, I don't take drugs, they can kill. I have plans to stick around and spend all this money I'm making."
Tim :	"Your songs sound as if you take drugs."
Karl:	"That's just singing, that's not real life. Real life is I just got married and I plan to settle down. Sounds boring? Don't you believe it."
Tim:	"Well, enjoy your stay in London and the tour. Best of luck with your new record and don't stay away so long next time."

- Cross out the inverted commas and write the conversation as a report:
  The interviewer said that ...

Basic Skills in English © Folens

Writing a report

A new bus service is being discussed in your neighbourhood.
You have been asked to carry out a survey into opinions and write a report.

- Use some of the phrases to report the four opinions from your survey.

- Use the chart below to help you write more sentences for your report.

He She They The...	added went on to say		that
	also	said thought pointed out	
in	his her Mr Smith's		opinion view

 • Turn over and write the report.

Basic Skills in English

Test your skills 1

- Divide the passage below into sentences and write in the punctuation.

 full stops

 'speech marks'

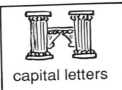 capital letters

 apostrophes

 commas.

i hate homework i cant see why we have to do it i just dont see the point in it if we need to do the work it would be much easier to work an extra hour a day at school its all very well for people with big houses or if they havent any brothers or sisters theyve got a chance of some peace and quiet i share my house with two brothers a baby sister my nan and granddad two dogs and my mum and dad he breeds budgerigars its only a three bedroomed terraced house the front room is my grandparents bedroom so what with all the people and the budgies noise i dont get much of a chance for peace

 NoW

- Go back and check your work with a partner.
- What kinds of mistakes did you make? Correct them.

- Below, write about what you think of homework.
- Think about: Would you rather work a longer day?
  Apart from leaving home, what can a person do?

Continue over the page ...

Basic Skills in English

© Folens

Test your skills 2

- Punctuate the conversation below.

 full stops    'speech marks'   capital letters   question and exclamation marks    commas.

are you going to the youth club tonight asked della

what for snapped hannah in reply there's nothing to do and people
stand around posing and smoking it's boring and i hate the smell

oh answered della there's no need to get so moody anyway i
thought you were going out with kris

going out thats another thing this going out business it's all daft no
one goes anywhere i like kris and i like talking to him but we don't
go anywhere just stand around breathing in dirty air i think id rather
go to the sports centre have a swim and then a coffee do you fancy
coming with me

della looked surprised then replied well i think you're right at least
the boys down there don't smoke

- Turn over and rewrite the conversation but put in your own ideas.
  Remember to start a new line each time a new person speaks.

- Go back and check your work with a partner.
- How well did you do?
- What kinds of mistakes did you make? Correct them.

Nouns are names

● Read the information about nouns. Complete the chart.

Type of noun	Definition	Examples	My three examples
Common nouns	Names of everyday things	cup bus	
Proper nouns	Names of people or places. They always start with a capital letter.	Africa Sarah	
Collective nouns	A name for a group of the same things.	a school of whales a flock of sheep	

 ● Underline the nouns in the paragraph below.

Bill was going on an adventure. In his rucksack he packed his binoculars, diving gear and hiking boots. He was touring Africa. Off the north coast he saw a shoal of red mullet and a school of whales. He stayed in Tripoli for a week. He travelled to Egypt to see the pyramids near Cairo and the Aswan Dam. Returning to Chad he hoped to see a herd of elephants and a pride of lions. Bill wanted to take lots of pictures with his new camera.

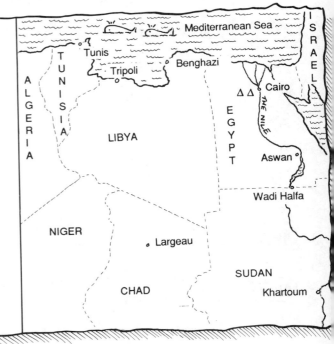

● On the map, mark in red the places that Bill visited.

Basic Skills in English   © Folens

Conjunctions

Conjunctions are joining words. They help to make better, more interesting sentences.

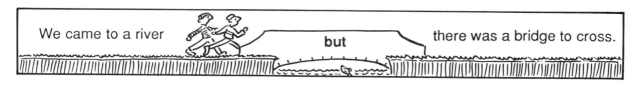

We came to a river **but** there was a bridge to cross.

therefore   since   unless   when   as

although   while   after   because   so

for   however   until   but   and

● Choose a conjunction to join the sentences below.

1. It was a really dark night _____ I had a torch and could see my way.

2. I had lost my wallet _____ I had to borrow some money to get home.

3. I cannot speak French _____ my mother comes from Paris.

4. The car was stuck in the snow _____ we always have a shovel in the boot.

Dean was skating well **BUT** he fell, lost points and came last.

The bus did not come **SO** I was late for school again.

● With a partner, decide how you would finish these sentences:

1. Chris was run over by a car and was sent to hospital although ...

2. My alarm didn't go off this morning so ...

3. All the shops in the High Street were shut because ...

4. We had booked a room in the hotel but ...

5. I hate swimming since ...

● Turn over and write five sentences of your own using conjunctions.

Sugar and spice ...

(...that's what little girls are made of).

● Look in the wordsearch for better words than *good* and *bad* to describe the twins.

NICE

CLUMSY

MESSY

DAINTY

MUCKY

KIND

PRETTY

CUTE

HORRID

SMELLY

NAUGHTY

Beautiful

z	v	f	s	u	o	s	w	w	t	m	n	z	m	p	s	f	n	o	j
x	d	a	i	n	t	y	w	l	p	u	z	q	w	r	i	e	h	u	r
n	l	jj	a	e	g	v	j	a	s	c	j	m	j	p	g	y	c	t	h
y	k	s	b	p	u	x	f	z	i	k	p	c	s	z	b	i	o	c	y
b	d	e	s	t	u	s	s	r	u	y	s	n	v	y	k	i	n	d	a
m	x	n	n	i	c	e	f	x	c	u	x	e	v	b	i	t	p	p	f
p	d	z	d	h	i	g	h	o	i	b	e	a	u	t	i	f	u	l	t
b	j	q	a	z	h	u	m	s	c	d	c	f	o	s	w	e	e	t	s
c	c	l	u	m	s	y	p	n	d	a	o	l	g	d	a	k	o	e	n
j	p	g	o	n	y	t	p	m	i	u	x	w	d	g	b	i	a	p	o
u	c	j	m	e	s	s	y	o	c	n	n	r	m	g	h	t	i	m	r
i	v	n	m	e	i	l	b	h	z	j	q	o	l	k	h	j	t	r	s
b	j	n	a	u	g	h	t	y	p	z	r	x	b	c	u	t	e	f	a
g	a	w	d	f	r	v	e	y	x	v	a	b	l	r	a	k	m	i	h
k	u	l	q	f	x	j	w	h	a	u	e	b	i	q	v	h	g	x	n
h	d	n	h	f	z	e	l	p	r	e	t	t	y	i	j	s	k	j	f
l	s	w	l	b	w	o	j	n	o	a	x	k	v	p	d	z	n	w	m
h	g	o	h	z	x	w	e	x	f	j	s	i	s	d	z	o	o	a	y
e	s	d	g	s	m	e	l	l	y	h	o	r	r	i	d	d	o	f	s
t	u	w	l	e	y	d	l	u	m	y	b	a	j	e	d	r	w	o	p

● What other words can you think of to describe them?

Slugs and snails and puppy dogs' tails...

(...that's what little boys are made of).

● Turn over and make a wordsearch to illustrate this proverb.

Basic Skills in English © Folens

Adjectives add interest

- Which of the two paragraphs below gives a better picture?
- Underline the describing words – the **adjectives**.

1. As Omar looked out of his bedroom window he saw the large, yellow sun rising into the clear, blue sky above the tree tops.

2. Omar looked out of the window. It was morning.

- Fill the gaps in the passage below.
- Choose adjectives from the lists or think of your own.

dark	pale
dirty	gloomy
rough	freezing
tatty	icy
fur	chilly
cloth	cold
woolly	quickly
older	slowly
taller	thin
large	white
small	pale
heavy	walked
light	trudged
metal	huge
iron	small
gold	big
wide	narrow

In the _____ light of the

_____ December morning the

_____ men faced the

_____ building. They wore _____

_____ clothing and _____ hats

with flaps to cover their ears. One man took a _____ ,

_____ bunch of keys from his pocket and unlocked

a _____ padlock from its chain.

- Add a second adjective to each description.
- Turn over and finish the story. What happened? Who were the men?

Adding colour

A verb tells us what someone or something is **doing**.
An adverb tells us **how** they are doing it.

verb	adverb
sings	loudly
walking	quickly

- Look at the passages below.
- Underline the **verbs** in red.
- Underline the **adverbs** in blue.

Tim's heart raced wildly as the car engine burst loudly into life.

He quickly leapt into the driver's seat. He crashed the gears badly and drove madly down the road.

The police car appeared suddenly and chased Tim. He drove blindly round a corner and had to brake sharply to miss a group of horse riders who were trotting carefully along the busy road.

- Imagine you are reporting the sports match shown in the two pictures below.
- Write your report. Who did what? How?

_____

_____

_____

_____

_____

_____

_____

- Underline the verbs and adverbs you have used.
- Talk about the differences you have made by using them.

Basic Skills in English © Folens

Adding colour 2

Adjectives add to a description.

● Read the letter below and underline the adjectives.

> *Dear Edna,*
>
> *I had to write to you. I am so thrilled with the lovely photos of our little Emma's wedding.*
>
> *I know I am her mum but she could be best bride of the year. Her new husband is a tall, good-looking chap with lovely white teeth and friendly manner. He also has masses of curly hair. He towers above my little girl who is so slim and tiny since she went to Weight Watchers.*
>
> *Her dress was made of cream crushed velvet with a calf-length skirt – to show off her little ankles and dainty feet. The veil was a heavy one in cream lace with a long train which had large, diamond-studded roses all over it.*
>
> *The pageboys were not keen on their matching strawberry pink outfits but that's boys for you. They liked their large hats complete with long pink feathers. Playing with the feathers kept them amused in church and at least they were well behaved.*
>
> *The bouquets were unusual as they were made up of winter flowers, it being a Christmas wedding. The holly leaves were a bit scratchy, though.*
>
> *I have enclosed photos. I can't believe that my lovely little baby grew into such a pretty bride.*
>
> *With love from*
>
> *Molly*

 ● Look at the pictures.
● Imagine you were at the wedding.
 Write to *your* friend. What did they really look like?

Describing objects

- Use the cards below to help you describe two everyday objects such as: a pair of scissors, a paper clip, a bicycle. One example has been done for you.

OBJECT:
Medicine bottle

COLOUR:
Usually brown

SHAPE:
Narrows at the top

SIZE:
Varies

TEXTURE:
Smooth

USE:
To hold pills or liquids

OBJECT:

COLOUR:

SHAPE:

SIZE:

TEXTURE:

USE:

OBJECT:

COLOUR:

SHAPE:

SIZE:

TEXTURE:

USE:

 NOW ☞ • Turn over. Use your notes to write a paragraph about each object.

Basic Skills in English   © Folens

Fill-em up!

You can make a story funny, happy or sad according to the words you choose.

- The story below is just an outline.
- Invent your people by drawing them in the spaces below.
  Are they kind or nasty? Are they hiding something?

- Decide what type of story you want. Choose suitable words from the lists.

interesting

frightening

sinister

kind

welcoming

generous

worrying

busy

quiet

small

popular

The shop was in a _____ in the High Street. It was
between a _____ supermarket and a _____
chemist shop. The shop had been there for years and had
always been a newsagents. When Mr Green died the place
was sold and new people moved in. At least they were a
family and were younger than Mr Green, he had always
been a _____ type of person. I like it when families
move into the area because I live _____ and we
can do with more young people. They were quite a large
family with _____ children, _____ parents
and _____ grand-parents. I delivered papers and
so I got to know them very well. There was something
_____ about _____ He/she
was always _____ .

understanding

funny

bossy

dancing

singing

shouting

fighting

mean

nasty

secretive

solitary

lonely

- Complete the story, making it more interesting.
- Compare your version with someone else.

Adjectives and adverbs

angry   reckless   shrill   violently

silent   ill tempered   surly   seething

• Fill the gaps below, using suitable adjectives and adverbs.

The _____ people were running _____ around the building trying to get in. The _____ police were hitting out _____ hoping to stop the _____ riot. One group of _____ boys was breaking the _____ windows of the _____ church on the corner while another _____ crowd was bouncing a _____ car trying to turn it over. The sound of sirens and _____ of gun fire was heard even above the noise of the riot. The police came in _____ numbers with riot shields.

• Compare your answers with a partner. What differences are there?
• Whose choices are better? Why?

 • Write a paragraph about each of the scenes below.
• Use the adjectives given.

lashed
howled
tore
screeched
uprooted
destroyed
overturned
battered
swept

clashed
scream
torn
up-ended
passengers
shocked
hurt
thundered
doctors
nurses

Basic Skills in English

Weather words

If you go on holiday and send a postcard home you might say,
'weather nice, lots of sun', or, 'weather rotten'.

● Look at the postcards below and write home describing what the weather
  is really like. Some words are given to help.

scorching

light

very hot

dry

sweaty

bright

gritty

heat

dusty

slippery

icy

fresh

bright

clear

blue

crisp

white

crunchy

Basic Skills in English

Similes

Similes are comparisons. They make descriptions more interesting.
A simile describes something using 'like' or 'as'.

● Underline the similes in the story below.

I went for a walk along the beach. The sand was as fine as silk and the grey rocks by the water's edge were like sleeping seals. The sky was as blue as a thrush's egg and the clouds were like wandering sheep. I felt as happy as a lark and I sang as I threw pebbles into the water and kicked the sand. It was such a lovely day – it was like heaven. I felt as free as the birds.

● Talk about how similes work.

Sandra is very thin and tall
... so you could say
Sandra is as thin as a rake!

● If you used the following similes, what would they mean?

My love is like a red, red rose.
My mum is as busy as a bee.
The wrestler on TV was a strong as an ox.

 ● Match the similes below to the pictures underneath.
The first one is done for you.

1. As pretty as a picture.
2. As good as gold.
3. As quiet as a church mouse.
4. As drunk as a lord.
5. As brown as a berry.
6. As stubborn as a mule.

     Basic Skills in English

Alliteration

Alliteration occurs when the first letter of more than one word in a sentence sounds the same.

● Read the examples below and then continue the list with your own sentences.

She sells sea shells on the sea shore.

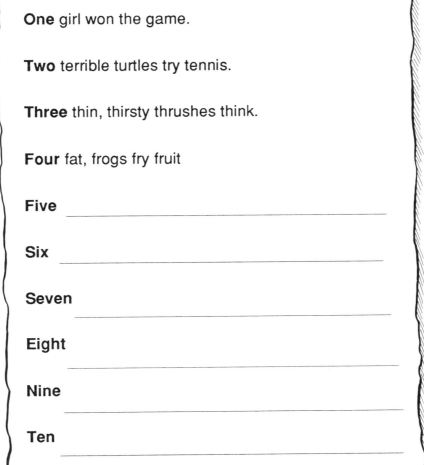

One girl won the game.

Two terrible turtles try tennis.

Three thin, thirsty thrushes think.

Four fat, frogs fry fruit

Five _____

Six _____

Seven _____

Eight _____

Nine _____

Ten _____

Peter Piper picks a peck of pickled peppers.

Round the rugged rock the ragged rascal ran.

Buy Ben's baked beans.

Advertisements use alliteration.
● Design some slogans. Look in the borders for clues.

diet
delectable
delicious
delightful
dishy

bursting
bubbly
blue
biological

fresh
foamy

clean
clear
crisp

shiny
silky
soapy

Dogfood _____

_____

Shampoo _____

_____

Washing-up liquid _____

_____

Basic Skills in English

Metaphors

Meta - what?

Tall, rugged, strong. This man is a mountain.

A metaphor is a way of comparing or describing something. It does *not* use like or as. It says something **is**. Sometimes this may sound strange!

Mrs Harrison **sailed** into the room .... (not walked!)
Her youngest son is a **drip** .... (not a boy!)

● Match the metaphors below to the pictures underneath.
   Explain what each really means.

1. My mother is a pillar of the church.	2. My goodness, it is raining cats and dogs.	3. Michael is a cabbage, he's such a bore.	4. Tim is a lion on the rugby field.

● Match the best endings to the sentences below.
● Underline the metaphors.

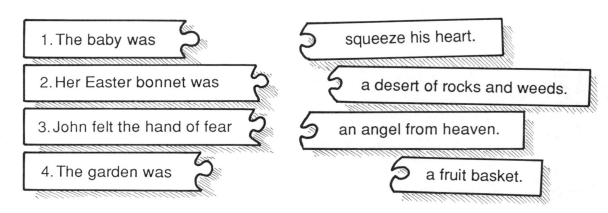

1. The baby was   squeeze his heart.

2. Her Easter bonnet was   a desert of rocks and weeds.

3. John felt the hand of fear   an angel from heaven.

4. The garden was   a fruit basket.

Basic Skills in English

© Folens

Which tense?

PAST TENSE	PRESENT TENSE	FUTURE TENSE
It has happened.	It is happening.	It will happen.

When you write a story you should keep it in the same tense (time).
- Underline the verbs in the three stories below and talk about the tenses they are in.

Yesterday was my birthday. As a treat I went bowling with some friends and then we went out for a hamburger.

Now I am sitting in the park having my lunch. My sandwiches have tuna fish in them and my mother knows I hate fish!

Tomorrow we are going to London to see the football at Wembley. I will stay overnight with my sister. She is a nurse and I will live with her one day.

- Write three paragraphs to practise each tense.
- Take your topic from the pictures and your tense from the word.

Yesterday

Today

Tomorrow

Put it right

- Read the passage below. There are some mistakes, not in spelling but in the grammar. Correct them. If you are not sure, look in the border for clues.

A teacher teaches - you learn.

Over there. Their clothes.

I can see. I have seen. A plant seed.

"That dog is driving me mad. I've got a really bad headache, you must learn that dog not to bark so much," Mum moaned as she went upstairs to try and get some sleep.

"Alright." I yelled back, Mum gets very cross with all the pets I've got. I put the puppy's lead on and taked him with me. I met my mate Jake and we went to the pet shop. We was going to go to the pictures but I was not going to ask Mum for money. The animals do make a mess but this puppy eated all mum's plants. Jake always makes me laugh, he telled me jokes all the way to the shops.

"Have you ever seed a Giraffe?" he asked me he reckons he has and I know it aint true because he hasn't never been abroad.

I buyed Mum another plant and tried to think of things to do to keep out of trouble. Jake knowed what to do and suggested we tidied up the garden. Me and him repainted the fence then asked Mum where she would like the new plant, as the part where the dog had been digging was bare she told us to put it over their.

Today I take the dog. Yesterday I took the dog.

Today you eat a cake. Yesterday you ate a cake.

I paint the fence. Jake paints the fence. Jake and I paint the fence.

I know. You know We all knew.

He was. We were.

Basic Skills in English

© Folens

Letter format

When you write important letters you need to follow rules.

- Using the clues below, write a letter to an electronics company to complain about a CD player you have bought.

Your address
Remember the postcode

Who is the letter for?
Complaints Manager
Skill CDs Ltd
Bendford
ESSEX ES1 2XO

Date

Dear,

I bought one of your CD players ...

Model?
Make?

It does not work. Does *anything* happen when I use it?

Do I want a repair, a refund or a new one?

I want you to sort it out.

Yours sincerely if you know a name. Mr ...?

Yours faithfully if you write to Sir or Madam.

Basic Skills in English

A holiday letter

Max was so excited about Italy that he blurted out all his news without thinking too much about the order. Can you sort it out for him?

- Cut his letter into strips and arrange it in the correct order.
- Can there be more than one version?

✂ —

Villa Marco Polo
Via Napoli
Castella
Napoli
Italia

— —

Dear James

— —

I am having a wonderful holiday with my grandparents.

— —

It was a bit hard at first but it soon becomes a habit. After all I sometimes talk to my dad in Italian when I am at home in England.

— —

The volcano, Vesuvius, is just behind the house.

— —

It's great to see all my cousins again and my aunts and uncles. They make such a fuss of me. I can do no wrong!

— —

My grandparents live in a little village near Naples, it's brilliant!

— —

My Granddad has promised to take me to see Pompeii because it is very near.

— —

I have to speak Italian all the time because the family here doesn't speak any English.

— —

July 29th

— —

The weather is great. It's hot and sunny and I never have to think about what tomorrow will be like. It never seems to rain in the summer.

— —

Rome is about 135 miles away but it's really easy to get there so we may go.

— —

We swim every day and I'm getting brown.

— —

Must go, see you as soon as I get home. Cheerio. Max

— —

Basic Skills in English   © Folens

In the wrong order

For a school project, Gary thought he would ask his Gran about what Christmas was like when she was young. Gary wrote notes but his Gran got things in the wrong order.

- Cut up the strips and rearrange the story. Think about each age group.
- Look at the pictures as a guide.
- Is there more than one correct order?

By the time your mother was born we had a television set. We were lucky. Then we moved down to the South Coast and it was years before you could get a picture down here.

Things have changed a lot. When I was a child we would get an orange for Christmas, if we were lucky we got a sugar mouse with a tail made from string. We always had a tree without lights; we made all the decorations to go on it.

When your mum was little I used to make her and your Auntie Jean a new dress and knit a new cardigan just to wear on Christmas day. Toys were very expensive and there wasn't a lot of choice. When Mum and Auntie Jean were little we always made the Christmas cake and pudding together and everyone had a go at stirring it and made a wish.

When I was a girl your great grandparents always made us go to church at least once each Sunday and we always went to midnight mass on Christmas eve. On Christmas day after dinner we all sat round the wireless (radio) to listen to the King's speech.

Anyway, by the time your mum was about 12 we had a television again. Christmas morning was spent opening the presents. They used to come and sit on our bed and open them. Then we had a big Christmas dinner – we always had lots of family around. Then we would sit round the television and listen to the Queen's speech. There weren't many programmes on then, not like now.

When Granddad and I were young we would go out carol singing, not just a few kids but big groups. If we were doing well we got invited into houses and they gave you drinks and hot mince pies.

Now everyone knows just what they want for presents, they get all the ideas from adverts and the cake, puddings and stuff can all be bought ready-made.

Correct it!

Your publisher has looked at the first draft of your story.
She says it is a good story, but she is confused.
You say 'we' and then 'they'.
You also say 'we will', 'we are' and then 'we did'.

- Read the draft, below. Underline the verbs.
- Decide if you are telling a story about yourself or another group of people.
  Choose the tense you want to use.

Tom and his friends are going on a walking holiday. We are going Youth Hostelling. They are planning their holiday and the route they will take. We don't want to walk more than 15 to 20 miles a day. They made a list of where the Youth Hostels are and are planning a route.

We made a list of the clothes we needed and the towels and bedding they will take. My Dad bought me some walking boots. My uncle said I would get blisters and should break them in first. He says I should put them on in the bath like footballers used to do. My Dad nearly has a fit and tells him not to be so stupid.

Mum made a list of all the meals we had and is planning a menu for every day. We bought our food each day so we won't have to carry so much. If we carry all our beans and bacon they won't be able to walk two miles never mind twenty.

We are buying foot cream, headache pills and indigestion tablets and they bought loads of plasters in case they got blisters.

The Youth Hostels are great. We had a kitchen to cook in and at night we sing songs and played games. We sleep in dormitories and in the morning before we left we had to tidy up. We have a smashing holiday and want to go again next year.

- Correct the story.

Basic Skills in English   © Folens

End of term report

- Read this report and:
  - underline in blue everything to do with attitude to work.
  - underline in red any comments on personal qualities.
  - circle any special features, such as giving pleasure or concern.

Name: *K Smith*
Class: *3B*   **Teacher:** Mr Barker

Subject	Grade	Comments	Initials
ART	C	He is co-operative in class, but does not have much ability. His sense of colour is all wrong. He lacks patience. He tries hard.	
BIOLOGY	C	He is bored. He does not like this subject and takes no part in classwork. His homework is poor.	
ENGLISH	B	He is interested in drama and writes with imagination. His creative writing is very promising, but his grammar and punctuation are poor. He reads a great deal.	
HISTORY	B	He is reluctant to take part in class. He reads widely about the subject but is quiet. His critical judgement is developing. A good student of history.	

  • Complete the chart below, using the information.

Attitude to work	Personal qualities	Special features
		Continue over the page ...

Basic Skills in English

Who is the murderer?

- Read the police files below.
- Tick the boxes in the chart if the facts fit the descriptions.

SUSPECT A

He is a butcher, so is used to knives. His clothes are often stained with blood. He is fairly tall, has dark hair, blue eyes and a beard. He is a strict family man with children. His wife is not allowed to go out except to church on Sunday and to the shops in the morning. He does not drink. He lives a quarter of a mile from Baker's Lane and he could have been in the murder area.

SUSPECT B

He is a professional boxer, is fairly tall and has black hair, a black beard and dark eyes. He appears all over the East End of London and is often out late at night. He carries a white cane, which is also a dagger, for protection. He dresses well because he says he must look successful. He does not drink and he runs every day to keep fit. He used to be married. His wife is either dead or has left him for another man.

SUSPECT C

He is the local doctor. He is fairly tall, well-built and dark with a beard. He is often out late at night, so people are used to seeing him. He is a good doctor and even performs his own operations when possible. He gets very angry when men get drunk and beat their wives and children. He often gives money to the poor mothers in the Baker's Lane area when the men have spent their money. He knows everybody in the area because he lives there.

FACTS CONCERNING THE MURDERER	SUSPECT A	SUSPECT B	SUSPECT C
Fairly tall and well built.			
Dark hair, beard and eyes.			
Could use a knife and had one.			
Could explain away bloodstains.			
Is religious.			
Is opposed to drink.			
Could have been there at the time.			
Could have written notes left with body.			
Would dress well.			
Could disappear easily.			
Knew the victims.			
Had a motive.			

 • Who do you think is the murderer?

Basic Skills in English   © Folens